WILD CATS

photographs by
Simon M. Bell

text by
Andrea Holden-Boone

SOMERVILLE HOUSE, USA
NEW YORK

ISBN: 1-58184-005-5   A B C D E F G H I J

Illustrated by Julian Mulock
Art Director: Neil Stuart
Design: FiWired.com
Printed in Hong Kong

Somerville House, USA, is distributed by
Penguin Putnam Books for Young Readers,
345 Hudson Street, NY, 10014

Published in Canada by
Somerville House Publishing
a division of Somerville House Books Limited
3080 Yonge Street, Suite 5000
Toronto, Ontario M4N 3N1

All photographs by Simon Bell with the exception of the
following: lion pride, page 10: Rick Edwards/Animals
Animals

The Publisher and photographer would like to thank the
following organizations and individuals without whose
help this book would not have been possible: Toronto
Zoo, African Lion Safari, Wildlife on Easy Street,
Northwood Buffalo and Exotic Animal Ranch; special
thanks to Pat Quillan, Norm Philllips, Wayne Jackson,
Dennis Kastner, and John Carnio.

CONTENTS

Words that appear in **bold** are explained in the glossary.

THE CAT FAMILY

The incredible cat — throughout human history, it has been worshipped, feared, and hunted. Cats outnumber dogs as the favorite pet in most households. Scientists believe the small cat became a pet when humans abandoned **nomadic** life and settled down into **stable** farming communities. Cats were valuable to early farmers because they hunted mice, rats, and other **vermin** that threatened to destroy the grain harvest.

Wild-Cat Families

All cats, wild or domestic, are **mammals** and belong to the family Felidae. Wild cats are divided into four groups. The first group includes domestic cats as well as small, wild cats like the ocelot, leopard cat, and sand cat. The second group includes big cats such as the lion, tiger, jaguar, leopard, and snow leopard. The cheetah and clouded leopard are each in a separate group. No matter what group cats belong to, they all have features that make them **uniquely** cats.

Ancient and Modern

Although *Felis catus,* the domesticated cat, can be traced back in time for about 7,000 years, the history of wild cats stretches back more than 34 million years. The earliest known cat is called *Proailurus.* Thought to have lived in the late Oligocene period, about 30 million years ago, it weighed about 20 pounds (9 kg) and lived mostly in trees. If time travel were possible, a visit to the late Oligocene would reveal many strange creatures inhabiting the Earth, but the *Proailurus* would be easily recognized as a cat.

The Famous Fossil Cat

By far the most famous of all ancient cats is the sabertooth. Its giant canine teeth were long, thick, and sharp, and extended well below its lower jaw. Many types of the sabertooth cat lived in various parts of Europe and Asia. Later, the sabertooth, or *Smilodon fatalis,* found its way to

▲ **This** domesticated **house cat shares many common behaviors with its wild relatives. Its body structure and methods of stalking, hunting, and eating** prey **are almost the same.**

▶ **This tiger (see Siberian tiger card) is beating the heat by resting in a shady spot. When night falls, it will be time to hunt, patrol his territory, and fend off intruders.**

North America. Fossil remains of the North American sabertooth cat have been found in the famous La Brea tar pits in California. It was nearly the size of a large lion and is thought to have hunted large animals like the **mastodon**.

Diminishing Populations

Humans have both feared and admired wild cats throughout history. Unfortunately, these great hunters have become the hunted — people's desire for furs and medicines has nearly wiped out some wild cat populations. Others have already become **extinct**. Now, governments and wildlife agencies are banding together to save wild cats and preserve some of the territory they need to survive.

▲ **The North American sabertooth cat's bones have been dated at more than 10,000 years old.**

5

CATS AND THEIR BODIES

3-D Margay Cat
3-D Geoffroy's Cat

C ats of all sorts are known for their sleek appearance, **agility**, and balance. Their skeletons and muscles have evolved over time into streamlined "moving machines." In order to hunt and catch prey, cats must be intelligent and quick — they must be able to leap, grab, and hold on to the animals they hunt.

Agile Bodies

A cat has a short neck and large skull. The eye sockets are deep and round to protect its precious eyesight and allow for a wide field of vision. Large bony openings for hearing and short powerful jaws equipped with sharp teeth are part of a cat's tools for survival. Long legs end in specialized feet that allow the cat to walk on tiptoe — very important for silently creeping toward prey and running quickly.

Most cats have narrow shoulder blades and a long **flexible** spinal column that extends into a tail. The tail is most often used for balance but a keen cat watcher also knows that a twitching tail can signal a cat's interest or playfulness. Cubs and kittens may follow a mother cat's uplifted tail through woods or brush.

▼ Funnel-shaped ears that amplify sound, big, light sensitive eyes, and a small, sleek, but powerful body make this margay an excellent hunter.

Teeth and Claws

The cat's teeth and claws are its most valuable assets as a **predator**. All cats, except for the cheetah, can **retract** their claws up into **sheaths**. The sheaths protect the claws from wear and tear, keeping them ready and sharp for hunting. Soft pads on the underside of the paws help the cat walk silently and provide **traction**. Each forepaw has five claws. The fifth claw acts like a thumb, enabling the cat to climb and grab prey. The hind paws have only four claws each.

Sight, Smell, and Touch

Cats have highly developed senses that allow them to be active at night. A special layer of cells called the **Tabetum lucidum** makes cat eyes six times more sensitive to light than human eyes. These cells can reflect and absorb the tiniest amount of available light, enabling cats to maneuver in the dark.

Even when a cat cannot see its prey, it can usually smell it. The cat has a keen sense of smell and uses both its nose and its mouth to pick up scents.

Whiskers are another handy cat tool. Whiskers (see oncilla card) are long, thick hairs extending out around the cat's nose and above its eyes and are connected to sensitive nerve endings beneath the skin. Cats can feel their way between branches and through dark tunnels by using their whiskers as guides.

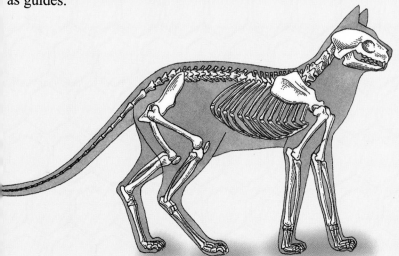

▲ A cat uses the special part of its mouth called Jacobson's organ to smell. Making a funny grimace (called the flehmen), this tiger pants, drawing air over the organ which picks up scents in the air.

◀ The cat's skeleton is strong and built for quick motion.

COMMON BEHAVIORS

W hether it is a mountain lion stalking a meal or a domestic cat on the prowl, cats have many similar behaviors. Watching the household cat closely as it hunts, plays, and grooms itself is not very different from observing a big wild cat go about its day.

3-D Geoffroy's Cat
3-D Clouded Leopard

Big cats have cubs, while small cats have kittens. When kittens and cubs are born, they are quite helpless. The mother cat will carefully tend to her brood for six months. She will teach them many things, including how to stalk, pounce, and kill prey. When they are very little, the mother carries her young in her mouth. It may look uncomfortable, but cubs and kittens are equipped with loose skin around their necks. Mother's method of transportation doesn't hurt a bit.

Sleeping

Humans think cats sleep a lot. In fact, they do — taking many catnaps during the day. Cats often rack up 16 hours or more of sleep. Sometimes they sleep with their eyes slightly open, on the lookout for possible danger. Big cats like the lion will rest for three or more days after a large kill, lying around with their **pride**, sleeping, grooming, and digesting their meal.

Hunting

The wild cat crouches low, moving very slowly, always keeping its eyes focused on its target. Cats instinctively attack the neck area of a hunted animal, aiming to kill quickly and efficiently.

Grooming

Cats, both wild and domestic, are known for their cleanliness.

The cat uses its rough tongue as a comb to clean and straighten its fur (see Geoffroy's cat). All cats lick their forepaws then run them behind their ears and over their faces. This action stimulates scent glands under the chin and rubs the cat's particular scent on its paws and legs. That way, the cat leaves its scent wherever it walks.

Marking and Sharpening

Cats are **territorial** — they stake claim by marking the ground with their scent. Trees, rocks, and bushes are favorite objects to mark. Big cats purposely leave **excrement** out in the open, giving notice to other cats that they may be trespassing on someone else's territory.

Roaring, Purring, and Hissing

Cats call to cubs and kittens, and possible mates. Big cats cannot purr but they can roar. Studies have shown that a lion's roar can be heard over five miles (8 km) away! A panther is known for its "scream." Small cats purr when contented, but they also purr when they are in great pain or distress. Perhaps the act of purring helps to calm them.

▲ Crouched low to conceal its body and walking silently on its tiptoes — this Geoffroy's cat is definitely on the prowl.

◀ A male lion has a powerful roar — he uses it to warn others off his territory, call for his pride, and show off his fierce teeth to a challenger.

9

KING OF THE CATS

3-D Lion
3-D Lion (cub)

Famous for its fierce roar and hunting **prowess**, the lion (*Panthera leo*) has always been a popular wild cat. Although lions (see lion cards) are not the largest wild cats, they are fierce predators that are not afraid of most animals in a few parts of India and on the **savannas** of Africa. As predators, lions play an important role in limiting the number of grazing animals that inhabit the plains. If herds of **grazers** were allowed to multiply unchecked, they would use up the grassland resources very quickly, making it impossible for any animals to survive.

A Social Animal

Lions are the only cats that prefer to live in groups, or prides. The pride can be large if there is abundant food, with up to 12 lionesses, 6 males, and the pride's young. There is one dominant male and one dominant female in each pride. Male lions fight for the right to mate with females and the stronger male either kills or chases away the loser.

Cooperation Means Survival

Lions help each other to survive. Lionesses are responsible for hunting and killing prey for the rest of the pride. The females work together to bring down large animals like the wildebeest that roam in herds across the savanna. The dominant female will often be the one to attack first while the others work to confuse and separate the intended meal from its herd. The lioness will first try to knock down the animal using her strong paws and body, then once the animal

▲ **Each member of the lion pride has a special position in the "pecking order." The dominant females and males eat a kill first while the others wait their turn for a meal.**

Keeping in Touch

Because lions are social animals, they tend to be the most **vocal** of all the cats. The male lion's roar is strong and powerful. In order to roar, the male lowers his head and arches its back at the same time. As the giant chest fills with air, the throat muscles tense. The sound emitted is a loud, deep, rolling growl that carries over many miles. The air from his lungs comes out with such force that puffs of dust rise from the ground several feet away.

is down, bite it in the neck to finish it off. Even though the females bring home the kill, the strongest male is allowed to eat first. Then the other males, in order of dominance, eat their fill. Lionesses eat next and cubs must wait till last.

Raising a Family

Lionesses cooperate to raise their young. About every two years, a lioness will have two to five cubs (the average litter is three). When young cubs are present, some lionesses will stay behind from the hunt to care for the babies. They hide young cubs in **scrub** or dry river beds. This way, the cubs are always protected, especially from their most threatening predators, hyenas, and strange male lions. When the cubs are old enough, after about a month, the lionesses will bring them to the pride. Cubs are allowed to nurse from any female in the pride — so if one is hungry while Mom is away on a hunt, the cub doesn't have to wait for a meal.

▲ This lion cub has much to learn in order to survive as an adult. At first, cubs practice stalking, pouncing, and catching prey by playing with other cubs in the pride. Later, they will follow and watch adults on the hunt for food.

◄ The male lion has a distinctive mane that makes it look large and fierce. Females have no mane.

SMALL WILD CATS

T he sand cat, black-footed cat, jungle cat, and domestic cat are members of the same family. All are classified as "small cats" and share many common behaviors. Small cats are not social like lions. They cannot roar, but tend to yowl or scream instead. And they can purr — something a big wild cat cannot do. Almost all are **nocturnal** and hunt many kinds of creatures including reptiles, birds, **rodents** and other mammals, and insects.

Sand Cat

The sand cat (*Felis margarita*) is one of the few cats that truly live in the desert. It is found in the Sahara desert, as well as desert areas of Asia. It digs **burrows** under sand **dunes** or scrub where it sleeps during the heat of the day and hunts at night.

The sand cat (see sand cat card) is small with an average body length of 20 inches (50 cm) and short legs. The sand cat's fur blends perfectly with its surroundings. The most common coloring is a light brown body with a black-tipped tail and red-brown streaks on the cheeks. The pads of its paws are completely covered with thick mats of fur to help it maneuver on slippery sand.

The sand cat can survive without drinking much water. It usually hunts desert rodents, hares, birds, reptiles (such as lizards and snakes), and insects. When it kills, the sand cat makes sure to consume its victim's body juices first, fulfilling its daily requirement of liquid.

▲ **This beautiful sand cat is strictly nocturnal. It lives in hot, dry desert areas and only hunts in the cool of the night.**

Egyptians painted pictures of the jungle cat, along with the African wild cat, on their monuments. **Archeologists** suspect that this cat was trained to hunt birds and other animals. Some of these wild cats were probably kept as pets. The jungle cat played a large part in Egypt's "cult of cats" and it is still a familiar part of Egyptian society.

Black-Footed Cat

Named after its black pads, the black-footed cat (*Felis nigripes*) is the smallest wild cat in the world. It inhabits dry regions of Africa, much like the sand cat. It weighs only an average of four pounds (2 kg) and has a rather short tail. Its fur is deep **ochre** with pronounced brown/black spots. Rings of black circle its legs, and the tip of its tail is also black.

Even though the black-footed cat (see black-footed cat card) is the smallest wild cat in the world, it is known to be fierce. Native peoples who live near its habitat tell stories of this tiny wild cat attacking much larger animals like sheep or goats.

Jungle Cat

The jungle cat (*Felis chaus*) is a small wild cat. Its coat ranges in color from sandy brown to brownish red. It almost looks as if someone has dipped it in ink because of the black tips on its ears and tail.

Don't go looking for the jungle cat (see jungle cat card) in your local jungle. Though its name might fool you, this small cat actually inhabits areas of Egypt, Israel, and Asia, and is commonly found in forested areas. Also called the reed cat, it often inhabits areas of tall grass and reeds near water.

▲ The flattened ears of this black-footed cat are a clear signal to stay away. Even though it is the smallest of all the wild cats, it has a big reputation for fierceness.

◄ Compare the size and markings of a domestic tabby cat on the left and a black-footed cat on the right.

MYSTERIOUS NORTH AMERICAN LONERS

3-D Bobcat

The bobcat and lynx are often confused because they look alike. The bobcat, however, inhabits almost every part of North America while the lynx lives only in the colder regions of Canada and Alaska.

Bobcat

Reclusive and fierce, the bobcat (*Lynx rufus*) is seldom seen. It will rarely come out into the open, and if it does, it is only for a fleeting moment. It lives in forest, desert, and swamp regions — anywhere there is ample food and cover.

The bobcat (see bobcat card) is about twice the size of a house cat. It is easily recognized by the **ruff** of fur encircling its face, its short ears, and its stubby four-to-six-inch (10 to 15 cm) tail.

▼ **During the 1970s, almost 92,000 bobcats were killed annually in North America for their fur** pelts. **They have survived, however, because of new laws protecting their** habitats.

While many wild cats have been hunted to near extinction, the bobcat has thrived. Although this cat will sometimes be hunted for its coat, its fur is not very highly prized. Its reclusive nature and adaptability have also helped it to survive. The bobcat easily outwits its pursuers, effectively disappearing into dense vegetation and eluding traps.

The bobcat is an adaptable hunter, feeding on over 40 different kinds of prey. If one type of prey becomes scarce, it is equipped to find other sources of food. It will eat only fresh meat — its favorite being rabbits and hares.

Canadian Lynx

Its numbers are unknown in Canada, but estimates suggest there are 300 to 700 lynx (*Lynx canadensis*) living in the United States. The Canadian lynx looks like a bigger version of the bobcat. The male lynx weighs 25 to 30 pounds (11 to 14 kg) while the female weighs 15 to 20 pounds (7 to 9 kg). Like the bobcat, it has a beard-like ruff of fur around its face. Its ears are tipped with spikes of fur that are a deeper color than its coat and it, too, has a short tail. The lynx lives as a **solitary** predator, hunting by day in the cold, forested regions of Canada and the upper United States.

The lynx provides a good example of a predator that mimics its prey. The staple of the lynx's diet is the snowshoe hare. Over time, the lynx has adopted long jackrabbitlike hind legs. Its powerful muscles mimic the hare's movement and its hind legs allow the lynx to leap 6 to 10 feet (1.8 to 3 m) with each bound.

▲ The lynx relies on the snowshoe hare for most of its food. It must catch and eat at least three snowshoe hares a week in order to live.

A Fine Balance

The lynx and snowshoe hare are closely connected. Studies have shown that, if the snowshoe hare population decreases, the lynx population will also decrease. Sometimes the lynx will hunt deer foundering in deep snow, or catch squirrels and grouse, but it is the snowshoe hare that is essential for the lynx's survival.

▲ Its huge paws, like those of the hare, act like snowshoes — they allow the lynx to travel and bound through deep snow without sinking.

SMALL AFRICAN AND ASIAN CATS

 Serval

 Caracal

▼ **The long** tufts **of fur on a caracal's ears can grow up to four inches (10 cm).**

I n Africa and Asia, many small cats have adapted to the harsh life of open plains and deserts. The caracal inhabits the dry, grassy, semi-desert regions of Asia and Africa. The serval lives near waterways on the plains. Other small wild cats, like the African golden cat and Asiatic golden cat, are found living in thick forests with dense vegetation.

Caracal

Caracal comes from the Turkish word, *Karakal*, which means "black ear." Like the lynx, the caracal (*Caracal caracal*) has tufts of fur that extend above each ear. Its coat is one solid color, usually a reddish brown. White fur grows underneath its chin, neck, and abdomen. The caracal (see caracal card) is smaller than the lynx, but has long, strong legs and an agile body.

Like most small cats, the caracal lives and hunts alone. Birds make up most of the caracal's diet. The caracal hunts and raids nests at dusk, but during very hot weather, it waits until full night. It is an excellent bird catcher. It can leap remarkably high, catching birds in midair with a powerful leap.

Trained caracals were used in India and Iran to stalk many types of birds and rabbits. The caracal hunted alongside humans, answering calls and following directions. Several caracals would hunt together; bets were often placed on the best cat — the one that could kill the most birds and rabbits.

Serval

The serval (*Leptailurus serval*) is a strange-looking creature because of its large ears and small skull. It is another small cat that purrs and growls instead of roars. It is nocturnal and lives alone. The average weight of a serval (see serval card) is about 35 pounds (15 kg) — the size of a small dog. It is long and slim with a **tawny** coat and dark spots.

Unlike the caracal, the serval is most often found near streams and the dense vegetation associated with them. Keen hearing and eyesight help it to track down prey. In fact, scientists believe that the serval relies more on hearing than sight to locate food in its **environment**.

African Golden Cat

The golden cat (*Profelis aurata*) is another small African cat with spotted fur. Its background color, however, can range from a dark brown to a bluish gray. It is about double the size of a domestic cat, with big paws, a small head, and a medium-length tail.

Asiatic Golden Cat

The Asiatic golden cat (*Profelis temminicki*) is closely related to the African golden cat. The Asiatic cat's rough coat can be a dark brown to a rich golden color. Some are spotted while others have only faint traces of spots on their fur. It is thought to live mainly on the ground, though some have been caught in trees. Birds make up its main diet, but this powerful little cat can also bring down small deer, sheep, goats, and calves.

▲ **This serval lives on the grassy plains of Africa.**

▶ **The Asiatic golden cat lives in the forests of Eastern Asia.**

17

OCELOT, MARGAY, AND GEOFFROY'S CAT

The ocelot, margay, and Geoffroy's cat are considered small wild cats that share the same **lineage**. Scientists have grouped them together because their skulls are all short and wide and they share a common tooth structure. Other cats included in this genetic line are the kodkod, oncilla, mountain cat, and pampas cat.

3-D Ocelot

3-D Geoffroy's Cat

3-D Margay

Ocelot

The ocelot (*Leopardu pardalis*) is small and secretive, preferring to avoid contact with humans. This small wild cat (see ocelot card) has a beautiful spotted coat with a background color that can be either a tawny yellow, red-gray, or plain gray. Its markings are unique. The ocelot's spots run into streaks that form **oblong** areas of shading. There are two black stripes on either side of its face and barlike marks that ring its tail. Dark spots mark its ears and neck.

Ocelots have been so over-hunted for their beautiful coats that they are now on the endangered species list. Only 50 to 100 ocelots still exist in the wilds of the United States. In addition, the forested areas where the ocelot lives have been cleared, making way for farmers and citrus growers.

Margay, or Long-Tailed Spotted Cat

In some parts of South America, the margay (*Leopardus wiedii*) is called the "little ocelot" because it so closely resembles its relative. The margay (see margay cards) has a beautiful coat with pronounced dark spots that have lighter centers. Unlike the ocelot, the margay is rarely found in the southern United States or Mexico. Its range is mostly through the middle of South America.

Like the ocelot, the margay is an excellent tree climber. Large paws and a long, strong tail help it cling to and balance on the branches of trees. The margay lives an almost completely **arboreal** life — it does its hunting, eating, sleeping, and mating high above the ground.

▲ Laws are in place that protect this beautiful, small wild cat, an ocelot, but its population is still struggling to survive.

Many small cats like the ocelot travel through their territories on frequently used "cat highways." They have regular routes they follow when searching for prey. For the ocelot and others, these cat highways can be interrupted by human highways. In Texas, for instance, many ocelots have been killed under the wheels of a truck or car. To combat this problem, the Texas Highway Department has begun to install culverts, or tunnels, that go underneath busy roads. Hopefully, the ocelots will learn to use them.

▲ This margay is so good at climbing that it can chase monkeys through the forest trees and make a successful kill.

Geoffroy's Cat

Geoffroy's cat (*Oncifelis geoffroyi*) is found in the mountains of South America, especially in areas of the Andes and mountainous regions of Argentina.

Like the ocelot and margay, Geoffroy's cat (see Geoffroy's cat cards) is a good climber and sleeps in trees. It preys upon small mammals such as rabbits, birds, rodents, as well as insects.

▲ The Geoffroy's cat is named after the French naturalist Geoffroy St-Hilaire.

19

GHOST CAT

The Puma (*Puma concolor*) was worshipped by Native Americans and feared by early settlers. They called it many names including "panther," "mountain devil," and "ghost cat."

3-D Puma

3-D Puma (cub)

▼ **The puma earned its nickname, "ghost cat," because of its** secretive **habits and solitary lifestyle.**

A Small Cat?

The puma, also called the mountain lion or cougar, is classified as a small cat, although it is the largest of them all. Males can weigh from 145 to 165 pounds (66 to 75 kg) while the females weigh 75 to 100 pounds (34 to 45 kg). The cougar has a loud purr, just like that of a domestic cat. But as wildlife observers have recorded, the cougar also emits a spine-tingling scream.

A Territorial Cat with a Huge Territory

Cougars are wanderers. They travel great distances in order to hunt and mate. Their territories can range from 8 square miles (13 square km) to over 500 square miles (804 square km). Male and female cougars mark their boundaries by scraping together piles of debris such as sticks and leaves, then spraying **urine** or depositing **feces** on top.

Because they are wanderers, cougars usually do not have **permanent** dens. They use caves, rock crevices, or dense thickets as **temporary** homes.

An Accomplished Predator

The cougar is a powerful cat that can hunt animals many times its own size. A powerful mass of muscle and **ligament**, the cougar is a strong and agile hunter — one of the most successful predators to inhabit North and South America. It is known for explosions of speed and is a stealthy **ambush** hunter. Big, strong hind legs give the cougar speed while it uses its front paws to steer. Its hind legs also allow it to leap to great heights, suddenly rising out of its cover to grab a meal. Deer is its favorite food, but the cougar does hunt many other animals as well, including elk, birds, porcupines, rabbits, sheep, and goats.

A successful kill means that the cougar can rest for a few days before it must hunt again. The cougar often drags a **carcass** some distance before it eats. When the cat has had its fill, it will drag sticks and leaves over the leftovers, attempting to cover them up. The cougar will then have a rest before it returns to feed again.

▲ This puma has a fur coat adapted to colder climates. Unlike that of its tropical relatives, his coat is longer and softer to keep him warm.

All cats, including the puma, belong to the scientific order Carnivora. Carnivores are animals that eat other animals for food. While it may seem cruel at times, carnivores play an important role in maintaining the balance of life. Pumas, for instance, feed mainly on deer. If no deer were ever killed, the herd population would increase greatly, making it difficult for any deer to find food.

▲ The care of the young (see puma cub card) is left to the mother puma. The male takes no interest in this chore.

3-D Snow Leopard

3-D Clouded Leopard

▲ This snow leopard mother guards her cub. After one year, the cub must be able to survive on its own.

Leopards exist mostly in Africa and some parts of Asia but they are still one of the most widely **dispersed** wild cats alive.

Leopard

Considered a big cat, the leopard (*Panthera pardus*) is the ruler of the forest. A leopard (see leopard card) can weigh up to 198 pounds (90 kg), making it bigger than a cheetah but smaller than a lion. It is the largest cat to climb trees easily and live a partly arboreal life. The leopard is mostly nocturnal, but will sometimes be active during the day. It has a sawlike call instead of a roar. The leopard's coat, usually yellowish orange with black spots, provides **camouflage** — the leopard can blend in with the sun-dappled leaves of its treetop environment.

The leopard goes after prey such as deer, antelope, monkeys, rodents, and birds. Sometimes it will scavenge a kill made by another animal. After killing a meal, the leopard commonly drags its prize up into a tree. The leopard usually wedges its meal into the fork of a tree to protect it from other **scavengers** like the hyena.

Snow Leopard

The snow leopard (*Panthera uncia*), sometimes called the "ounce," inhabits the high, cold, mountainous regions of Asia and Siberia. An extremely beautiful cat (see snow leopard card), the snow leopard is also very rare and secretive. It is not a true leopard but its creamy white coat is similarly marked with dark spots. The snow leopard's fur is very thick, helping it to survive in its harsh habitat.

Unlike other cats, the snow leopard is active in the daytime. It hunts mountain goats, sheep, ibex, birds, and rabbits. The snow leopard's den might be a rock **crevice** or cave, and it is usually used over and over again. Sometimes snow leopards are seen resting in abandoned vulture nests.

Clouded Leopard

The clouded leopard (*Neofelis nebulosa*) is not considered a true leopard either. In fact, scientists have placed it in a group of its own since they cannot agree whether it is more closely related to the puma or the big cats. The clouded leopard is rather small, weighing an average of 49 pounds (22 kg). Its coat is brownish-gray with dark, elongated spots. The clouded leopard's very long tail is marked with rings, and, since it is a climbing cat, its tail helps it balance.

The clouded leopard (see clouded leopard card) lives in the dense forests of southeast Asia and is very difficult to spot or track in the wild. Most scientists believe that the clouded leopard rarely comes down from the trees, making it more arboreal than any other large cat. Most clouded leopards live and hunt alone, though they sometimes remain in male and female pairs. In any case, these cats keep scientists guessing with their mysterious behavior.

A "black panther" is really a leopard. Unlike most cats, leopards have a melanistic or black color phase which is caused by **recessive genes**. A litter of leopards can have both normal-colored and melanistic cubs in it.

▼ This clouded leopard slinks through thickly forested areas in search of prey which includes wild pigs, goats, and monkeys.

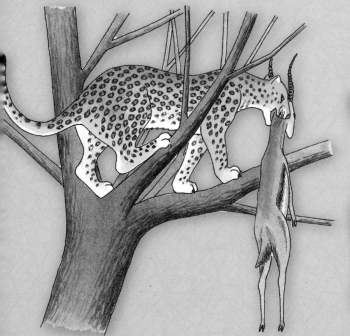

▲ Because it can haul an animal many times its own weight, we know how strong and skillful a leopard is.

23

THE BIGGEST AMERICAN CAT

3-D Jaguar

▼ **Jaguars have an odd habit of burying their kills, returning later to feed.**

People often mistake the jaguar (*Panthera onca*) for the leopard — but the leopard lives in Africa and Asia while the jaguar can be found only in the Americas. The largest American cat, the jaguar (see jaguar card) lives primarily in the tropical forests of South America. It once inhabited parts of the southern United States as well, but much of the jaguar's habitat has been eroded by human development. To make matters worse, ranchers and farmers used to kill this big cat because it attacked livestock. The jaguar has also long been hunted for its beautiful coat. Recently, because of protection laws, a few have been spotted again in the United States.

The jaguar is the only American cat scientifically classified as a big cat. The male has a body length of up to 7 feet (2.13 m) and a tail of 21 inches (53 cm). The jaguar is a powerful cat, with a large skull, paws, and teeth. It has a beautiful spotted coat that ranges from a pale yellow to reddish brown. The spots form **rosettes** with a dark ring surrounding a lighter center. These spots help the jaguar camouflage itself against the sun-dappled background of the forest while it stalks its prey. Its long tail is marked as well and usually ends in a black tip.

A Powerful Hunter and Swimmer

Often the jaguar is found near the edge of forested waterways: rivers, swamps, and marshy areas. The jaguar is not afraid of water. It swims often and occasionally even fishes. Jaguars have been observed smacking their paws into water and flipping out large, squirming fish for dinner.

A Tropical Buffet

The jaguar sleeps by day and hunts by night: most of its hunting takes place on the ground at dusk and dawn. Jaguars are not picky eaters. In all, they eat over 85 different species of animals — a diet that has helped them survive in an ever-declining habitat. Jaguars climb trees to chase and kill monkeys and **sloths**. Jaguars also stalk river turtles that are laying eggs. They hunt the turtles, then dig up and eat the eggs as well. But the jaguar's favorite meal is the wild pig, or javelina. In South America, these pigs travel in herds and a jaguar is usually not far behind the herd.

Explorers in South America mistook the jaguar for a tiger or panther. Latin American peoples called it *yaguara*, or "wild beast that overcomes prey with one bound." Others gave it the name *yaguarete*, which means "body of a dog." In other areas it is called *tigre americano*, or the American tiger. Today, most of Spanish-speaking America calls the jaguar *El tigre*.

▲ Another staple of the jaguar's diet is the biggest of all living rodents, the capybara. It lives in groups along the sand banks of large rivers.

▶ Because of their weight, jaguars cannot chase prey up into the higher, thinner branches of trees. Monkeys, and other animals flee from a menacing jaguar by climbing above the jaguar's reach.

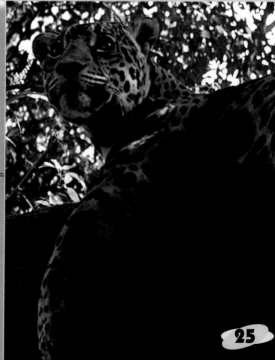

THE BIGGEST WILD CAT

3-D Siberian Tiger

The biggest wild cat in the world is the tiger (*Panthera tigris*). Sometimes called "the great hunter," it has also become the hunted. These awesome cats are in grave danger of extinction. More Siberian tigers now live in zoos than in the wild.

Tiger Facts

The tiger has a huge, powerful body, large paws, and massive skull. Bengal tigers can weigh up to 573 pounds (260 kg) and some species of Siberian tiger (see Siberian tiger card) weigh even more. Its jaws are extremely powerful and the tiger can often kill prey with a single bite to the neck. The tiger's hind legs are longer than its forelegs. This enables it to

▼ Tigers are definitely at the top of the non-human food chain in their environment. They do not fear any animals, except for other tigers and humans. They are solitary predators.

The White Tiger

White tigers are born, every so often, due to recessive genes. Instead of an ochre coat with black stripes, this white tiger has a snowy-white coat marked with black stripes. While the white tiger may be a popular draw at the zoo, it is thought that the white coloration may make it more difficult for survival in the wild. It does not camouflage itself as well as the yellow tiger, and may have a more difficult time stalking prey undetected.

pounce on and ambush prey. Strong, muscular forelegs allow the tiger to grip its prey, sometimes breaking the animal's neck before the tiger bites.

Somewhat Social

Unlike lions, tigers do not live in social groups. They have vast territories or ranges that may sometimes overlap. Female tigers usually have set boundaries that are smaller than male tigers' ranges. Just as other wild cats do, they mark their boundaries with urine and feces to warn other tigers away. A male tiger's range may include several smaller female ranges. Tigers found in groups usually consist of a mother and her cubs. Sometimes, however, tigers will band together if food is scarce. They might share a kill, but the tiger's hunting method and habitat are better suited to solitary life. Females alert males that they are ready to mate by emitting a special scent.

A Water Cat?

Of all the big cats, the tiger is most at home near or in the water. Tigers frequent the edges of waterways, preying on other animals that are drawn to drink. The tiger also swims for pure enjoyment. In hot, steamy jungles, swimming is an effective method of cooling off. The tiger is a strong, powerful swimmer. Any animal that thinks it can outwit a tiger by leaping into the water is in for a big surprise.

▲ Tigers love to swim and swim very well. This tiger is not afraid to chase prey into the water, and it also swims to cool off when the heat of the jungle is too intense.

◀ A tiger's stripes provide excellent camouflage when it hunts or rests.

27

CHEETAH: THE FASTEST LAND MAMMAL

3D 3D Cheetah (cub)

The cheetah (*Acinonyx jubatus*) is in a class by itself. It is unlike any other cat, big or small, and has habits and **adaptations** uniquely its own.

A Living Sports Car

Cheetahs are known for their amazing bursts of speed when on a chase. A standing cheetah can accelerate from zero to 45 miles per hour (72 km/h) in just two seconds. During a longer chase, cheetahs have been clocked at speeds of 70 miles per hour (112 km/h) or more. Although amazingly fast, this cat can keep up that kind of speed for only a few hundred yards.

A Body Built for Speed

Cheetahs have long, slim bodies with long legs and tails. Although the cheetah does not climb trees, the tail helps the cat balance when making fast turns. Its claws do not retract into sheaths like that of other cats but stay exposed at all times. The claws are blunt and slightly curved, much like a dog's. This gives the cheetah good traction when running at high speeds. Strong muscles and a flexible spine allow the cheetah to make long, powerful strides while running.

Raising the Young

A female cheetah can have one to eight cubs (see cheetah card) at a time. The mother tends to her family diligently, nursing for many weeks and then

◀ Unlike other wild cats, cheetahs are able to run down prey at high speeds. They have narrow paws with blunt claws that provide traction.

bringing meat to the cubs once they are old enough to chew it. The cubs are born blind and helpless like other cats but, within two weeks, are quite active. Often, the mother cheetah joins their running and pouncing games. As the cubs mature, they go with her on the hunt but usually watch from a high vantage point while Mom chases down prey. Then, when the kill is made, they join her in feeding. Cubs stay with their mother almost two years before they go off on their own.

▼ **This cheetah commands an excellent view from a termite mound.**

▲ **This cheetah cub faces a** precarious **future. Its population has been hunted so extensively that most cheetahs now exist in protected range parks or in zoos.**

It is thought that cheetahs are far-sighted. They often find a high spot on the plains, possibly a termite mound, and view the land around them for a possible meal. In zoos, it has been observed that a cheetah will often bump into objects that are in close range. It's almost as if the cat cannot see what's right in front of it, but can spot even the subtlest motion occurring far away.

29

STEREO PHOTOGRAPHY

Our Eyes

A pair of eyes is one of the most complex systems found in nature. Scientists don't fully understand all the intricate mechanisms that allow humans and animals to see. Scientists do know, however, that both eyes work together with the brain to form images that have three dimensions: length, width, and depth. Viewed through only one eye, everything appears flat, or two-dimensional. Using two eyes allows humans to perceive the third dimension — depth.

How the Eyes Work

Because our eyes are a few inches apart, each eye sees a slightly different angle of the same object. The information from each eye is carried by nerves to the brain. Then, in a process called fusion, the brain forms a blended image that is three-dimensional. Fusion allows humans to judge distances between objects, and determine how far away they are.

How a Stereo Camera Works

Stereophotography works like human eyesight. The most sophisticated stereo cameras have two lenses about the same distance apart as human eyes. Two images are taken simultaneously, each with a slightly different angle of the same object. When both images are viewed through a special viewer, called a stereoscope, the two images are blended together to become one image that has three dimensions.

Eye-to-Eye™ Books

This Eye-to-Eye™ book contains cards with paired images of wild cats taken by a stereo camera. When you look at the cards through the stereoscopic viewer, a 3-D image is formed in your brain. This is because the left side of the card mimics what the left eye might see, while the right side mimics the right eye's perspective.

To View the Cards

Carefully remove the viewer from the front of the book. Lift flap and insert tab. Carefully remove the cards from the back of the book. Insert cards one by one into the slot. When you have finished viewing the cards, store the viewer and cards in the pocket on the inside back cover.

Simon M. Bell specializes in stereographic nature photography and is founder and president of BPS, a multimedia studio based in Toronto, Canada.

Simon began shooting pictures at the age of six when his father gave him a "Brownie" box camera.

GLOSSARY

Adaptations - changes or adjustments that enable something to fit different circumstances.

Agility - the ability to move swiftly and easily.

Ambush - a surprise attack made from a place of hiding.

Arboreal - living in or among trees.

Archaeologist - a person who studies ancient societies and the way of life and the customs of their people by digging up and studying their tools, pottery, weapons, household items, and the ruins of their buildings.

Burrows - holes, tunnels, or openings dug in the ground by a small animal such as a rabbit or mole.

Camouflage - the natural coloring of an animal that enables it to blend in with its surroundings and hide from predators.

Carcass - the dead body of an animal.

Challenger - one who invites an opponent to take part in a contest or fight to see who is the better, stronger, or faster.

Crevice - a narrow opening resulting from a split or crack.

Cubs - the young of such animals as bears, wolves, or lions.

Dispersed - moved or scattered in different directions.

Domesticated - trained to live with and be useful to human beings.

Dominant - most important or powerful; ruling; controlling.

Dunes - hills of sand that have been made by the blowing of the wind.

Environment - the surroundings in which a plant or animal lives.

Excrement - waste matter discharged by the body.

Extinct - no longer in existence.

Feces - bodily waste discharged through the anus.

Flehmen - grimace made by a cat when it is analyzing a scent.

Flexible - open to change or new ideas.

Grazers - animals that feed on growing grass.

Habitat - the place or kind of place where an animal or plant usually lives or grows.

Ligament - a band of strong tissue that connects bones or holds organs in place.

Lineage - one's descent in a straight line from an ancestor.

Mammals - animals that have four legs, fur or hair, and the ability among females to produce milk for their young.

Mane - the long hair that grows from the neck and head of certain animals.

Mastodon - an animal that looks very much like an elephant. It lived thousands of years ago.

Nocturnal - of the night or happening at night.

Nomadic - roaming about from place to place aimlessly or without a fixed pattern of movement.

Oblong - longer than broad or round; rectangular with adjacent sides unequal.

Ochre - the pale, brownish-yellow color of impure iron ore.

Pelt - an animal skin with the hair or fur still on it.

Permanent - lasting or meant to last for a long time.

Precarious - dangerous; having a lack of stability or security that threatens with danger.

Predator - an animal that lives by killing and eating other animals.

Prey - an animal caught or hunted by another animal for food.

Pride - a company of lions.

Prowess - extraordinary ability; distinguished bravery.

Recessive gene - a gene that does not produce a characteristic effect but tends to go back to a latent inherited characteristic.

Reclusive - having a tendency to withdraw from society.

Retract - to draw back or in, as cats can do with their claws.

Rodent - any of several related animals such as a mouse, rat, squirrel, or beaver.

Rosette - an ornament, object, or arrangement shaped like a rose.

Ruff - a growth of fur or feathers that looks like a collar around the neck of an animal or bird.

Savanna - a tropical or subtropical grassland containing scattered trees and drought-resistant undergrowth.

Scavenger - an animal that feeds on garbage or other dead or decaying matter.

Scrub - vegetation consisting mostly of stunted trees.

Secretive - not frank or open.

Sheath - a case or cover of an animal body part.

Sloths - animals of tropical regions. Sloths live in trees and hang upside-down from the branches with their claws. They move very slowly.

Solitary - existing or living alone.

Stable - not likely to go through sudden changes in position or condition; fixed; steady.

Tawny - of a warm sandy color like that of well-tanned skin.

Temporary- short lasting or used for a short time only.

Territorial - of or restricted to a particular region.

Traction - the friction that keeps something from slipping or skidding.

Tufts - bunches of grass, hair, feathers, threads, or other flexible materials that grow or are held tightly together at one end and are loose at the other.

Uniquely - without like or equal.

Urine - a clear or yellow-colored fluid containing body wastes.

Vermin - insects or small animals that are annoying or destructive or harmful to health.

Vocal - of or made by the voice.

Entries in *italics* refer to photographs and illustrations.

INDEX